WINNING

God's

WAY

Colossians 3:23

ROD OLSON

CROSSTRAINING

PUBLISHING

Winning God's Way

Rod Olson

ISBN 1-929478-59-3

Cross Training Publishing
317 West Second Street
Grand Island, NE 68801
(308) 384-5762

This book is manufactured in the United States of America.

Library of Congress Cataloging in Publication Data in Progress.

I wish to dedicate this book to the Master Coach and architect of my life, my Lord and Savior Jesus Christ. The principles he left us are truly timeless and life changing. I would also like to thank my wife, Marla for all her patience and love as a coaches wife and mother. This book would not have been possible if not for the vision of Frosty Westering, the ministry of Scotty Kessler and Wes Neal, the steadfastness of Kirk Talley and the unselfishness of Johnny Square. I would also like to thank Derek Fullmer and the Colorado FCA staff for all their prayers and support. Finally, I want to thank the Air Force football staff for inspiration and all the players over the years that I have had the privilege to coach, this is for you, thank you.

C O N T E N T S

WEEKS 10-12

"LEAVING A LEGACY AS AND ATHLETE, FRIEND & PERSON"

GROUP COVENANT

I, _____

Commit with my Winning God's Way group to do the following:

1. Complete the Winning God's Way worksheet each week before the group session.
2. Pray regularly for my fellow group members.
3. Participate in all group sessions unless urgent circumstances beyond my control prevent my attendance.
4. Participate openly and honestly in the group sessions.
5. Keep confidential any personal matters shared by others in the group.
6. Be patient and compassionate with my fellow teammates and my school as we grow closer to God and see how He wants us to serve.
7. I will pray for my school, my coaches and my teammates at least one time per week.

OTHERS YOU WILL BE COMMITTING TO PRAY FOR:

_____

_____

_____

Signed:_____

Date:_____

WINNING GOD'S WAY GROUP MEMBERS:

_____

_____

_____

_____

_____

_____

WINNING God's WAY

O UTLIN E

WEEK 1 —GET WIRED—JOHN 15:5
"Are you a Christian-athlete or a Athlete that is a Christian?"
➤ The purpose of this lesson is to assess where you are as an athlete both in and out of the athletic arena.
CROSS REFERENCE: Romans 8:28

WEEK 2—THE TRAITS OF A LEGACY BUILDER—TITUS 3:1-2
"What it takes to be the Real-Deal!"
➤ This lesson will focus on being a servant, messenger and "a sent one." We will embrace the fact that in order to be the greatest, you must become the least.
CROSS REFERENCE: Mark 10:43-45

WEEK 3—COMMITMENT TO EXCELLENCE—MATTHEW 6: 19-25
"What are my goals and how do I reach them?"
➤ The purpose of this lesson is to discern Godly goals from worldly goals for a Christian athlete, and to help the athlete understand how to reach and measure those goals.
CROSS REFERENCE: Colossians 3:23-24

WEEK 4—FEEDING THE MONSTER—MATTHEW 25: 14-30
"Is your schedule/sport eating you up...reset your priorities!"
➤ This lesson will focus on time management. We will discuss what a Christian-athlete's priorities look like and how a student-athlete can maintain balance within a hectic schedule.
CROSS REFERENCE: Matthew 6: 33-34

WEEK 5—TAMING THE TONGUE—JAMES 3: 1-12
"Living a 'Playah's' lifestyle...the way God wants!"
➤ The purpose of this lesson is to help the athlete 'talk the talk & walk the walk' of a Christian-athlete on a daily basis.
CROSS REFERENCE: Ephesians 6:10-20

WEEK 6—SEED PLANTERS—PROVERBS 22:6
"Kids may not listen to parents or teachers, but they will listen to their Friends!"
➤ This lesson will focus on the calling that we have in our friendships as Christian-athletes for the kingdom of God.
CROSS REFERENCE: John 5: 17

WEEK 7—CHECK YOUR OIL—I TIMOTHY 5:21-25
"Character and Motives...Making wise choices in difficult situations"
➤ This lesson we will discuss the type of character and motivation God would like Christian-athletes to possess. We will also discuss the implications of character and motivation on a athlete's ability to make Godly choices and decisions.
CROSS REFERENCE: I Corinthians 10:13

WEEK 8—THE DATING GAME—1 THESSALONIANS 4:3-5
"Character and Motives...Making wise choices in difficult situations"
➤ This purpose of this lesson is to help the athlete learn what God has to say about dating and sex in today's world and to also give the athlete biblical principles and practical ways to handle the pressures of dating and sex.
CROSS REFERENCE: 2 Timothy 2:22

WEEK 9—BREAKFAST OF CHAMPIONS—1 CORINTHIANS 6:19-20
"To supplement or not to supplement, that is the question"
➤ The purpose of this lesson is to discuss the use of supplements as a Christian-athlete and to also help the athlete develop a biblically based process for determining whether or not they should use supplements.
CROSS REFERENCE: 2 Corinthians 7:21

WEEK 10—MISSION POSSIBLE!—PROVERBS 19:21
"God's Purposes vs. Our Plans"
➤ During this lesson we will discuss what God's purpose was in creating athletes and coaches. We will also learn how to align our plans with God's by utilizing the "Double Win" philosophy.
CROSS REFERENCE: Philippians 2:13

WEEK 11—HE IS CALLING YOU OUT!—PHILIPPIANS 2:12-18
"Will you be a athlete God can use—Any way He wants?"

➤ This purpose of this lesson is to show the importance of being obedient to God, in regard to the calling we have as both a Christian and as an athlete. We will also discuss how one Player can impact the world!

CROSS REFERENCE: John 10:3-5

WEEK 12—GET IN THE GAME!—ISAIAH 49:6
"More is Caught than is Taught!"

➤ The purpose of this lesson is to give the Christian-athlete practical and useful ways to leave a legacy for the kingdom of God in regard to style of play, improving team chemistry, leading bible studies among your team, and servant leadership activities on your campus and in your community.

CROSS REFERENCE: Matthew 28:19-20

| WEEK 1 |

GET WIRED!

*"Are you a Christian-athlete or an
Athlete that is a Christian?"*

READ: John 15:5

I. THE SOUL (READ JOB CHAPTER 42)

You can tell what is recorded on a person's soul by the way he/she reacts
to _____. Even though Job was under great adversity and was
shocked by comments from friends and family, he never responded in a
negative fashion.

When your integrity has been questioned, how have you responded?

Are you a Christian-athlete or an Athlete that is a Christian?
What is the difference?

II. THE BODY

Our body _____ says a great deal about how we respond to difficult
situations. Throughout scripture many of God's leaders/athletes chose to
walk-away or not react to volatile situations in a worldly way even though
others were urging them to respond. (WWJD?)

Do you think before you act?

Do you compete the way Jesus would compete, how would He compete?

What kind of messages do you send with your body language and style of play?

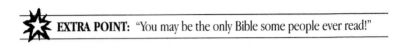

EXTRA POINT: "You may be the only Bible some people ever read!"

III. THE SPIRIT

The Spirit of God knows the true _____ of a person's heart. God will use tough situations to draw your intentions out. (Discuss tough situations i.e., poor officiating, trash-talking opponent, coach chewing you out etc...)

HOW TO TAKE ACTION: The Word of God is the "Mechanism" that allows God speak to you on how to handle tough situations. The next time you find yourself in a difficult situation remember Romans 8:28 "And we know that in all things God works for the good of those who love him, who have been called according to his purpose." Then ask yourself...what would Jesus do? And do it!

MEMORIZE: Romans 8:28

THE TRAITS OF A LEGACY BUILDER

"What it takes to be the 'Real Deal'!"

READ: Titus 3:1-2

I. THE ATHLETE/PERSON

We have always heard coaches preach that there is no 'I' in TEAM. Just as a coach looks for _unselfish_ players, God looks for us to be _servant_ leaders on his team.

Leaders lead the way by going first, by going further and by giving maximal _sacrifice_ _effort_ . Jesus Christ was the perfect 'servant leader'.

Are you the most important person on your team or are your teammates?

How do you model Servant Leadership to your team/friends?
(Examples: Picking up equipment, getting water for other players, doing the dishes or a chore that is not normally your responsibility, etc.)

II. THE EQUIPMENT

Just as a player must be equipped properly to be safe and perform
optimally, God has equipped us, his servants with all the 'state of the art'
equipment necessary to be great servant leaders in today's athletic world.
He has given us a playbook called the Bible . He has given us a Mentor
in JC , and finally, he has given us teammates and coaches that
we can disciple and teach with in our walk as Christian servant leaders.

What is your most valuable piece of equipment and Why?

III. THE CHALLENGE

The challenge God puts before us is to set aside our selfish needs and
serve him. In order to do this as athletes we must trust God, not try
to control Him. We must be obedient to God and properly utilize the
equipment he has entrusted to us.

HOW TO TAKE ACTION: Instead of focusing on what you want, focus on
helping others, especially younger players. When defining your goals focus
on long term instead of short term. Treat every player the way Christ would
treat them. Envision what you want your team to look like 10 years from
now. Next, visualize what type of legacy you want to leave the players of the
future, and finally envision what you will say when God asks you how you
did as a leader and role model for him at your school and in your
community.

MEMORIZE: Mark 10: 43-45

WINNING God's WAY

WEEK 3

COMMITMENT TO EXCELLENCE

"What are my goals and how do I reach them?"

READ: Matthew 6:19-25

Jer. 9:23-24

I. THE PURSUIT OF EXCELLENCE (WORLDLY VS. GODLY)

As athletes we love to set goals, such as a start every game, win a conference championship and or win the state championship. We are in awe of championship rings and news clippings. We compete for trophies, individual honors, and perhaps a scholarship or more! But God tells us He wants us to focus on __Godly__ goals. Goals that can't be __stolen__ , rust or fade away. He wants us to compete to His glory and store up __treasures__ in heaven. He wants us to compete for an __eternal__ significance.

MAKE TWO LISTS: Worldly personal Goals & Godly personal Goals *(Examples: Win a Title, be All-American **and** Align my plans with God's purpose)*

Worldly - selfish
Become rich
popular
toys
power

Godly - selfless
descipleship
witness
grow closer to him
help others

Write what you think God's list of goals would look like for you:

God's List of Goals '4' Me

short ⟨ 1)
       2)
long ⟨ 3)
       4)

II. YOUR TRAINING REGIMEN

As athletes, we know that if we want to reach our maximum potential we must train every day without exception. As Christians, we must train everyday in the Word and Prayer, if we are to reach our 'potential' as Godly athletes. You have seen the results of an athlete that trains religiously every day, why not let God train you for 30-60 minutes a day so you can maximize your potential!

Do you block out time to train with God on a daily basis?

Are you coachable-meaning, do you have a great attitude and give great effort in spending time with God?

HOW TO TAKE ACTION: Make time for God. Schedule daily appointments with God for devotions and prayer in your day-timer or PDA. Write them in! Make sure you are visiting with God in a location where you will not be distracted and be sure that you are meeting with him at a time of the day when you are refreshed and ready to meet him.

MEMORIZE: Matthew 6:6

FEEDING THE MONSTER

"Is your schedule/sport eating you up...reset your priorities?"

READ: Matthew 25: 14-30

I. TALENTS AND GIFTS

At some point in your life someone told you that you are a gifted athlete and or you have a bright future in athletics. Those statements most likely propeled you into athletics.

Think back and please write (below) why you started playing sports?

Have your reasons for playing changed? If yes, please state how.

II. TIME - (GREAT PLAYERS CREED: "LEAVE NO STONE UNTURNED...")

There are ___ hours in a day, ___ hours in a week and _____ hours in a year.

Your _____ determine how you utilize the time God has given you.

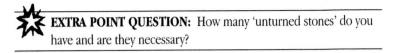

EXTRA POINT QUESTION: How many 'unturned stones' do you have and are they necessary?

Please list your priorities in order of importance?

This is how God would like your priorities to look...How does your list match-up?
1. Your Personal Relationship with Jesus Christ (Faith)
2. Your Family
3. Your Education/Friendships
4. Your Sport

III. BALANCE

God can do more in 6 minutes than a person can do in 6 months. God is the ultimate _____ and has perfect _____. If we hope to achieve balance in our lives we must have our _____ in the proper order and God will honor our _____. If we are not right with God and close to him he cannot guide us, and if He cannot guide us we will be at the mercy of a chaotic world.

HOW TO TAKE ACTION: Look at your priorities above and try to narrow them to four. Next, across from each priority list the number of hours per week you put towards each one. Pray to God on a daily basis to help you utilize your time wisely for the kingdom of God and to keep your priorities in order. (If you are a group leader or captain, ask your peers to list their priorities and time commitments and see if you, as a group leader, are allowing them to be productive people in God's kingdom.)

MEMORIZE: Matthew 6: 33-34

TAMING THE TONGUE

"Living a 'Playah's' lifestyle...the way God wants!"

Read: James 3: 1-12

I. THE TALK

A person's _____ displays what type of _____ he or she has.

Do you build players/people up or tear them down?
What does it mean to 'speak greatness' into someone?

EXTRA POINT: "A good coach tells a player what he can do, not what he can't do."

II. THE POWER OF THE 'PUT-UP' (A SINCERE, SPECIFIC COMPLIMENT) GAME

'Put-Ups' keep us _____ positive and hopeful. 'Put-Ups' keep us free from the negative power of _____ shifts.

(Example: "Colt, that is the best pressure defense I have seen anyone play since I have been a player here. You have come a long way and you are going to be a great player here!")

Describe a situation when someone said something negative to you that you have never forgotten. What type of an impact did it have on you?

Describe a situation when someone spoke greatness into you. What type of impact did it have on you?

III. THE WALK/THE BATTLE (READ EPHESIANS 6: 10-20)

Your daily walk as a Christian-coach in today's world is a _____.
Satan does not want you to succeed as a Christian-athlete. You are in a _____ and your _____ speak louder than your _____!

How would your teammates describe you?

How would your greatest adversary describe you?

HOW TO Tame the Tongue and Walk the Walk:
Have a clean heart. Ask God to renew your heart and to guard what you say everyday. THINK before you speak. Is what you are going to say True, Helpful, Inspiring, Necessary and Kind? Next, surround yourself with Godly people, if none are available, ask God to send someone into your life.

Finally...be slow to speak...and quick to listen!

MEMORIZE: Proverbs 29: 20

SEED PLANTERS

*"Kids may not listen to parents or teachers,
but they will listen to their Friends!"*

READ: Proverbs 22:6

I. YOUR CALLING

In a world where quick results and fast food are the norm, the Christian-athlete is called to do _____ than just win games. We are called to _____ seeds of hope in the _____ of tomorrow. We are called by God to share our _____ through words and actions with our teammates, with a hope that someday the seed will take hold, develop strong roots, grow and give them _____ life.

Do you feel that your actions in competition can influence others toward Christ? Why and How?

II. THE FIELD

Just as a farmer must till the soil before he/she can plant the seeds, a Christian-athlete must realize the power the field of play possesses. _____ is one of the few environments that allow for so many opportunities to teach and model the type of behavior God wants in all situations. What a great _____ and _____.

Are you tending your playing field with the type of responses God wants?

III. THE HARVEST (READ MATTHEW 9:37-38)

If a planted seed isn't _____ and fed by the farmer and nature it
will ____. As leaders, it is not enough to just plant the seed of faith through
our actions, we must share what God is doing in our lives with others. And
just as the farmer trusts God to bring rain, we too must _____ God to
work in the _____ of others as they watch us and we pray for them.

How much care do you take in the seeds you sow?

Are you praying for God to help you share your faith in action and word?

HOW TO TAKE ACTION: Ask God for courage to share your faith, and
pray for your teammates daily. Especially pray for the ones with which you
are having problems. Look for teachable moments and don't give up.
Remember, some seeds take longer to sprout than others.

MEMORIZE: John 5:17

CHECK YOUR OIL!

"Character & Motives...Making wise choices during difficult situations"

READ: John 8:1-11

I. THE OIL (CHARACTER)

Coaches in the South have a saying when it comes to measuring a player's character; they call it 'checking his oil'. As coaches and players, we often question other players' or a colleague's character at the drop of a hat; however, Christ tells us to look at our own _____ before pointing the finger at others.

How would players in your league describe your character?
How would the parents of other players describe your character?
Do you like their perception? If not, how can you change it?

II. THE FUEL (MOTIVES)

If the fuel in a vehicle is not _____ and _____, the engine will not respond properly and will eventually sustain damage. Our hearts are not much different. If our motives are not _____ and _____ when making decisions, we too will eventually sustain damage to our lives and possibly to those around us.

Think of a time when you had to make a difficult decision-what were the motivating factors that lead you to your decision? (i.e., winning etc.)
Did you consult your Father in Heaven? If so, why?

III. POOR DECISIONS + TEMPTATION = WEAKENED CHARACTER

Many players think they lose a game based upon one bad decision or play, but most of us know that usually it is a series of small mistakes that slowly causes defeat. Satan is no different; he looks to attack our _____ spots and _____ areas first, in hopes of slowly weakening our character until it cracks. As Christian-athletes we must protect ourselves by utilizing _____ wisdom and by maintaining pure and Godly motives when making decisions.

What are some of the ways you can protect yourself from making poor decisions? *(Examples: No snap decisions, have an accountability partner, being in the Word...)*

HOW TO TAKE ACTION: The next time you are tempted or in a difficult situation think of, I Corinthians 10:13, and remember God will not permit you to be tempted more than you can stand and when you are tempted, pray and He will give you a way out so that you will be able to make a good decision.

MEMORIZE: I Corinthians 10:13

THE DATING GAME

"Sex and Sports"

Read: I Thessalonians 4:3-5

I. FRIENDSHIPS AND RELATIONSHIPS

As Christian-athletes, we are very cautious about who we choose as friends. We only want people around us that will help us reach our potential, not friends that will put us in potentially harmful situations. Dating should be no different. If we are going to date, we must _____ consider if that individual has similar _____ and _____. If he or she does not, it will be very difficult for both people to handle sensitive situations like maintaining self-control when being tempted to engage in premarital sex. (Read 2 Corinthians 6:14-18)

What is your motivation for dating and what type of individual do you think God wants you to date?

II. HOW FAR IS TOO FAR? (READ MATTHEW 5:28)

Every game has boundary lines. These lines are there to _____ the players and to keep the game from getting _____. When dating, individuals must _____ and pray with each other to establish Godly boundaries for their relationship so they don't get out of control.

The Bible says that anyone that looks at a woman lustfully has already committed adultery with her in his heart. Lust isn't just our sexual appetite; it is that out of control desire that causes us to sin. Paul writes in Romans 14:21, that we should be cautious not to do anything that could cause another person to lust. So in a dating relationship, each person should be careful not to do anything that would cause the other person to lust. But how far is too far? Learn your date's level of what causes he/she to lust through _____. Talk and pray about it. That may be tough, but real relationships require communication and prayer.

What do you think God thinks is too far?

IV. ACCOUNTABILITY

A good coach can help a player learn to handle the pressures of a game by sharing his/her past experiences or by just listening and coaching. In a dating relationship, there will be many pressures and it can be very beneficial to have a married Christian couple close by to help coach you and your date through the many pressures of dating at a young age. Consider them to be your relationship coaches!

Memorize: 2 Timothy 2:22

BREAKFAST OF CHAMPIONS

"To supplement or not to supplement...that is the question!"

Read: I Corinthians 6:19-20

I. BIGGER, FASTER, STRONGER!

As Christian-athletes we know we are to treat our bodies as a _____
and to abstain from alcohol and drugs, but what about taking a legal,
natural supplement that can enhance my workouts and body? Technology
has made the athlete's nutritional choices very difficult at best. As athletes,
we all want to be bigger, faster and stronger, but as Christian-athletes we
must _____ God and remember He has _____ for us (Jeremiah
29:11), regardless of how big or fast we are.

Do you think God wants you to take legal supplements to enhance your
athletic performance? Why or Why not?

II. JESUS, THE HOLY SPIRIT AND CREATINE

When Jesus played ball on earth (and He did!), do you think He would have
taken a supplement such as creatine? Paul writes in first Corinthians that
our bodies are a temple of the Holy Spirit. The Holy Spirit actually

_____ in our bodies! That means our bodies are _____ and should be treated with respect and _____. As Christian-athletes we believe Jesus would have chosen to be _____ filled rather than supplement filled.

Are you honoring God by feeding your body the spiritual calories it needs everyday? How?

III. GOD AS YOUR PERSONAL TRAINER (READ PROVERBS 23:19-20)

The only way you can make the right choices in nutrition is to use God as your personal trainer and the Bible as your nutritional guide. You must be _____ and keep your heart on the right _____.

 EXTRA POINT: If it is not of God it will not be honoring to God.

HOW TO DO IT: Before ever considering taking a nutritional supplement seek God's guidance in prayer and His Word. In addition, consult with your family doctor, your coach and your parents. You have only one body, and remember God has great plans for you, regardless of your size, strength or speed! TRUST HIM!

MEMORIZE: 2 Corinthians 7:1

MISSION POSSIBLE!

"God's Purposes vs. Our Plans"

READ: Proverbs 19:21

I. SCRIPTING FOR SUCCESS

Our coaches spend countless hours preparing game plans, practice plans, and even contingency plans. But sometimes even the best plans fail. As the Master Coach, _____ has written a flawless game plan that has a specific purpose for each one of us. It is our calling as Christian-athletes to see what His _____ is for us and align our _____ with His purpose.

What do you think God's purpose is in having you as a player on His team? *(Example: He wants me to be his point guard and lead others to Christ.)*

II. GOD'S PLAN FOR ATHLETES AND COACHES

Have you ever wondered why God created athletes and coaches? Ask a few other athletes and your coach for their thoughts and write their responses below.

READ: I Corinthians 9:22-23

Athletics is a microcosm of life. It mirrors life's situations in the arena and on the field. Sport gives us opportunities to display how God wants us to handle success and failure. As Christian-athletes, we believe God created athletes and coaches to demonstrate great _____ and to _____ the weak.

III. FOLLOWING GOD'S GAME PLAN (I CORINTHIANS 9:24-27)

As Christian-athletes, God wants us to maintain a 'Double Win' philosophy. In other words, God demands that as His players we must _____ _____ and strive for the _____ that is set before them. We should strive to win on the scoreboard and in _____, specifically _____ life.

EXTRA POINT: Consider writing a mission statement for yourself, as a player in God's kingdom.

HOW TO MAKE SURE YOUR PLANS ALIGN WITH GOD'S PURPOSE for YOU: The next time you are not sure if you are doing what God wants you to do:
1) Be still, pray and ask God for clarification. (Fasting, keep your antenna up!)
2) Read the Bible.
3) Seek Counsel from other Godly people (perhaps outside the situation)
4) Proceed and look for affirmations from the Holy Spirit in people, the Bible and circumstances.

NOTE: Remember, if it is not of God it is not from God.

MEMORIZE: I John 2:17

HE'S CALLING YOU OUT!

"Will you be an Athlete God can use — Any way He wants?"

READ: Philippians 2:12-18

I. ORDINARY PEOPLE EXTRAORDINARY THINGS!

More games have been won through the efforts of _____ athletes than all the famous athletes combined. More people have come to Christ through the efforts of _____ people than all the famous evangelists combined!

Ask yourself; will I be an athlete God can use?
Will I be an obedient team player and let Him use me any way He wants?
What do these questions mean to you? What keeps us from being obedient?

II. IT ONLY TAKES ONE!

How many times have you had a coach tell you that if just one of the players on your team would just step out and raise their level of play it would _____ all the other players around them? We see it everyday in athletics, one person with a _____ and a purpose takes their game to a higher level and their _____ inspires their teammates to do the same and consequently, together everyone achieves more (i.e. Michael Jordan).

God wants to use you to inspire others for his kingdom, what are some ways you can be useful to God as an athlete? *(Example: Living out your faith through the way you compete in athletics, actions speak louder than words...)*

III. IMPACTING THE INFRA-STRUCTURE

An apple _____ from the inside out and usually by the time you notice, it is too late. Players, coaches and teams are not any different. That is why God has _____ you to 'impact the infrastructure', by giving your teammates and opponents the love and knowledge of _____ that they need to be solid individuals in the game of life.

What happened to Jonah when he didn't go to Nineveh? (If you don't know the story of Jonah, read Jonah Chapter 1:1-17)

EXTRA POINT: "It only takes one player who is obedient to his/her calling to inspire others. If you are obedient it frees God to do great things!"

HOW TO 'IMPACT THE INFRA-STRUCTURE': Sell out to putting the kingdom of God first and winning second. Winning is a by-product of aiming for perfection in Jesus Christ. Realize that God uses ordinary people to do extraordinary things. He wants to use you, just let him!

MEMORIZE: Colossians 3:23-24

GET IN THE GAME!

"More is Caught than is Taught!"

READ: Isaiah 49:6

I. CLINIC TALK

Have you ever been to a camp for your sport and the information you received from the speakers and coaches was just fabulous; but as you returned to home and began to implement the concepts into your workouts, it just wasn't as easy as it sounded? In other words, you loved the concept and what it could do for you, but you needed more specific details and instructions to make it fit into your style.

That is the purpose of this lesson—

To begin, just jot down any questions you may want to bring up for discussion.

II. IMPACTING PLAYERS/TEAM — "CREATE MEMORABLE EXPERIENCES"

You can impact your teammates and opponents on a surface level by the way you play or with short conversations, but you can change your teammates and opponents lives forever by letting them experience being a servant-leader first hand and by you and your coaches creating memorable experiences. Always look for teachable moments!

Examples: Waiter/Waitress Day in the cafeteria, Drink servers at fast food restaurants, pump gas at local gas stations, operation blessing to other teams, 12 ways to bless your opponent, and lastly a "quality use of a waste of time" — just being together... whether it is an FCA huddle or just a team night that is not related to your sport.

III. GO DEEPER! ATTEND FCA LEADERSHIP CAMP! MENTOR SOMEONE OR COACH A YOUTH TEAM! — "MORE IS CAUGHT THAN IS TAUGHT"

Christ chose 12 and went even deeper with 3 of the 12. If we are to further the kingdom of God we must do it the same way Christ did...multiplication... one person at a time.

Examples: Ask God to rise up one or two individuals that you can mentor for a semester. It could be a young elementary school or junior high athlete. Agree to meet once a week to read the Bible or just hang out.

IV. GET IN THE GAME! — GET INVOLVED!

You will never know until you've tried. You have the time just keep your priorities in order..but remember God's kingdom comes first.

Examples: Lead an FCA huddle on your campus, go to an FCA camp, start monthly servant leadership projects at your school or in your community, see where God is working and join him!

MEMORIZE: Matthew 28:19-20

A N S W E R K E Y

WEEK 1
1. ADVERSITY
2. LANGUAGE
3. INTENTIONS

WEEK 2
1. UNSELFISH
2. SERVICE
3. SACRIFICE
4. BIBLE
5. JESUS CHRIST
6. DISCIPLE
7. TEACH
8. SERVE
9. TRUST
10. CONTROL

WEEK 3
1. GODLY
2. STOLEN
3. TREASURES
4. ETERNAL

WEEK 4
1. 24
2. 168
3. 8,736
4. PRIORITIES
5. PLANNER
6. TIMING
7. PRIORITIES
8. FAITHFULNESS

WEEK 5
1. TONGUE
2. CHARACTER
3. MENTALLY

4. MOMENTUM
5. BATTLE
6. FIGHT
7. ACTIONS
8. WORDS

WEEK 6
1. MORE
2. PLANT
3. ATHLETES
4. FAITH
5. ETERNAL
6. ATHLETICS
7. CALLING
8. RESPONSIBILITY
9. NURTURED
10. DIE
11. TRUST
12. HEARTS

WEEK 7
1. FLAWS
2. PURE
3. CLEAN
4. PURE
5. CLEAN
6. BLIND
7. VULNERABLE
8. GOD'S

WEEK 8
1. PRAYERFULLY
2. VALUES
3. BELIEFS
4. PROTECT
5. OUT OF CONTROL
6. COMMUNICATE

7. COMMUNICATION

WEEK 9
1. TEMPLE
2. TRUST
3. PLANS
4. DWELLS
5. HONOR
6. SPIRIT
7. WISE
8. PATH

WEEK 10
1. GOD
2. PURPOSE
3. PLANS
4. CHARACTER
5. CHAMPION
6. WORK HARD
7. PRIZE
8. LIFE
9. ETERNAL

WEEK 11
1. ORDINARY
2. ORDINARY
3. INSPIRE
4. VISION
5. PASSION
6. ROTS
7. CALLED
8. JESUS CHRIST

WEEK 12
NO ANSWERS NEEDED

NOTES

STUDY LEADER'S GUIDE

DEAR WINNING GOD'S WAY STUDY LEADER,

Thank you for furthering God's kingdom by choosing to spend time with your athletes in a mentoring fashion. By accepting this call and challenge, you align yourself with the many followers of Jesus Christ who have listened to his call and agreed to commit to further His kingdom. As a Winning God's Way study leader, you may never completely know the impact you have for the kingdom until we all get to Heaven and are with the Father, but at that time it will be clear to all! The Winning God's Way study mentoring series is a twelve-week series, predicated upon one meeting each week for thirty to seventy five minutes each session. We have found that it is best in a one on one setting, but can be very beneficial when used with small groups of athletes of ten or less. The lessons are very simple and short and are to be completed prior to the meetings. As the facilitator, group discussion and interaction is crucial. I would also like to encourage you to pray earnestly to God before you begin the mentoring process with a young athlete. It is imperative that both parties involved are committed to the mentoring process. To insure that God is working in the mentoring process and that both parties are committed for the right reasons, I would encourage you, as the mentor to ask the athlete to commit to three weeks of meetings, at that time you both will evaluate and pray if it is beneficial that you continue the process. I would again encourage you and your athlete to reevaluate again, after six total weeks. If at that time, you and the athlete feel good about the relationship and growth, and that God wants you to continue for the remaining six weeks, there is no need for further evaluation, only commitment.

In closing, I would like to encourage you to hold your meetings in a place that is private and confidential. But I would also remind you that more is caught than is taught. Which means, invite your athlete to your home so he or she can see what it means to be a Christian as a parent, spouse or adult. Therefore, I encourage you to be faithful with a little and to be patient with yourself and your group. It is not up to you to change people's hearts...that is God's job. It is your job to share the word of God and the biblical principles included in this study and God will do the rest. Remember, the Word of God never comes back void!

May God bless your efforts and may you follow God's direction.

In the Master Coach's name,

Rod Olson

WHY A WINNING GOD'S WAY STUDY?

The Winning God's Way study series came from God and was developed to fulfill a need for coaches to have a relevant Bible study. I wrote Winning God's Way to fulfill a need for athlete's/teams to reach their potential through a mentoring processs with their coach for the Fellowship of Christian Athletes Coaches Ministry in Colorado. Several years ago, God brought a man into my life named Scotty Kessler. As a head football coach at the collegiate level, I brought Scotty in as a consultant to assess our football program and coaching staff. Through those meetings God used Scotty to teach me how to integrate Biblical principles into my coaching philosophy and program. My life was changed forever, as I finally had been given the knowledge and tools I needed for God to use me to minister to coaches and athletes through my coaching. As I went deeper in my relationship God, I found myself being called to the ministry with the yearning to tell others how coaching with Biblical principles changed my life! However, one of my biggest struggles as a Christian coach, was finding

Bible studies that were relevant to my career as a coach. Surely, Jesus had something to say to a person that worked for a nickel an hour, 80 to 90 hours a week, was paid to win, and had hundreds of people that would listen to and believe anything I said! And besides, I needed to know what Jesus had to say about handling an angry parent or getting fired! Needless to say, I didn't find any studies in the bookstores that dealt with those topics. After visiting with Johnny Square (chaplain for the Colorado State University football program) I decided to ask God to help me put on paper just a few of the principles I have been taught and that have allowed me to become close enough to God so that he may use me to leave a legacy for His kingdom through coaching. This mentoring series came out of a need that coaches expressed in wanting to mentor their student-athletes with relevant materials that met the student-athlete's needs and questions.

YOUR WINNING GOD'S WAY GROUP

You are going to find an eager group of athletes in your weekly meetings. You are going to find that this study crosses all gender, race and sport. Players and coaches from all different levels and sports are going to enjoy great prayer time and fellowship while they learn. Every person wants to know how they can get closer to God, and every Christian athlete wants to know how they can be a Christian and still compete and win according to God's glory! You are going to have a ball!

If you are a first time group leader or inexperienced group leader, you will enjoy the leadership guide and short lessons. Everything is based on the word of God and each lesson begins and ends with scripture. As Paul said, "My speech and my preaching not with persuasive words of human wisdom, but in demonstration of the Spirit and of power, that your faith should not be in the wisdom of men but in the power of God" (1 Corinthians 2: 4-5).

All you have to bring to the table each week is a willingness to serve God and others, the truth of God's word, and a total dependence upon God to do His work.

As you pray each week for those things and God's guidance, you will hear athletes share stories about what they have learned and how God is working in their lives. You will see lives transformed and you too will grow closer to God. Finally, as you finish the study with your group you will see the power of God move, as your group members want to continue meeting and start their own Winning God's Way study groups with other athletes. And that is what leaving a legacy is all about! Praise God.

GROUND RULES FOR YOUR SMALL GROUP

To ensure that everyone in your group is on the same page, I would encourage you to lead the group in making 3 commitments:

1) Everyone agrees to and completes the Winning God's Way group covenant sheet located at the beginning of the study booklet. You don't need to collect the sheets but everyone should fill one out for their own level of commitment.
2) Everyone commits to spending time prior to meeting in preparation for the lesson. This is not a difficult task as the lessons are short and the answers are located in the back of the booklet.
3) Everyone commits to ask God to change their lives according to the Biblical truths presented.

THE STRUCTURE OF EACH WINNING GOD'S WAY LESSON

Each week, God leads athletes through a dynamic, life changing process through the lessons. Each lesson begins with a topic and scripture that ties to that specific topic or principle. There are fill in the blanks along with questions to facilitate thought and discussion. Finally the lesson, concludes with a "How to take Action" section which gives the athlete practical tools and steps for how to implement the principle taught that day into their daily routines. But most importantly, each lesson concludes with scripture that is again relevant to the lesson's topic and the student is expected to memorize the verse or verses. Memorization is a key part of the weekly lesson as the Word of God is the sword of the Spirit.

DISCUSSION LEADER'S GUIDE

HOW TO START A WINNING GOD'S WAY GROUP:

Get copies of the Winning God's Way books, and show a copy to the players you would like to meet with. Ask them to glance at the study and see if they would be interested in spending time together talking and learning about God. Your group can be athletes from any sport or any level and can be a male or female. The only criteria you may want to stand firm on is that they are or have been an athlete. The optimum sized group would be eight to twelve assuming that some student-athletes may have to miss occasionally. Decide that you will meet for 12 weeks at a consistent time and location, preferably a room that is a private setting, but comfortable. We have found that evenings are a great time for student-athletes to meet, as there are minimal conflicts. But many coaches have met over the lunch hour and have found it beneficial, just make sure to leave 15 minutes for eating prior to the lesson. If the group gels, you can continue to meet and move to the 2nd study in the Winning God's Way volume 2 from Cross Training Publishing (www.crosstrainingpublishing.com).

WEEK 1:

Have water or soft drinks available if possible. Set up the room so that you are all sitting in a circle or at least around a table. It is important that everyone can have eye contact. If you are meeting over lunch, allow fifteen minutes to eat and then begin the meeting. Distribute a copy of the Winning God's Way Mentoring study booklet to each member. Go over the twelve-week schedule in regard to start time/finish time and meeting place. I would also encourage you send a sign up sheet around with email and phone number information in case a meeting must be cancelled or postponed due to inclimate weather. Briefly discuss the Winning God's Way Group Covenant in the beginning of the booklet and encourage them to fill it out and keep it in their books. Next, tell them that each meeting will begin with you asking them to share what is going on in their lives and how the group can pray for them. Every meeting will begin with fellowship, sharing and prayer. This is vital and cannot be missed. It may be difficult at first, but be patient and let God work. Assign the first lesson as next week's assignment and ask them to be prepared to share if necessary. Next, go around and ask each person what sports they play and what their favorite food is, also have them share some information about their family. This is a great way to break the ice and get to know each other on a more personal level. Be sure to point out that we are here to support and encourage one another and not convict each other. Lastly, close with a prayer and always start and adjourn on time! Many times, individuals must leave early to get to school on time, just make sure they understand that is fine and any information they may have missed they can get from a colleague or yourself. Lastly, have fun...this should not be work!

TYPICAL WEEK:

Each week begin with each person sharing what is happening in their lives and any prayer requests they might have, you are to go last. As the facilitator, you are going to be the one praying following the requests so I would encourage you to have a spiral notebook that you write the person's name and prayer request in for each meeting. This will allow for two things: One, you will be able to keep track of the requests and petition all of them to God that day, and two, you will have a log at the end of eleven weeks of everyone's prayer requests and if you like at the end you can separate each person's prayers and share with them how God answered their prayers and others.

- Fellowship/Sharing & Prayer requests   20 Minutes
- Weekly Winning God's Way Lesson   30 Minutes
- Closing Group Prayer   10 Minutes

ALTERNATIVE TO TYPICAL WEEK:

Prepare to let the fellowship/sharing and prayer time go where God wants it to one meeting. Or if something has happened in the media that is of merit for discussion in regard to athletics or today's youth, prepare a 20-minute discussion and facilitate it, finishing with prayer.

I would encourage you to wait at least 4-5 weeks into the lessons before doing this, so you have more of a biblical base for the discussions. Also, I would not do this more than once as the series is twelve weeks long and you don't want the weeks to get to long.

LEADING A LESSON/DISCUSSION:

The key to a successful meeting and group discussion is your ability as the leader, to insure that you keep a delicate balance between each group member having the opportunity for input and making sure the material in the lesson is covered adequately for learning to occur. Your role is to keep the meeting moving while encouraging each person to render his/her thoughts on the subject that day. If questions come up that are off the subject, simply suggest that we discuss that at another time. If someone tends to dominate the dialogue (including you) privately, ask them to help you draw out the more introverted members of the group. If you have a shy member, tread lightly, but ask them every so often, "_____, what do you think about this question?"

You don't have to be a graduate of a seminary or an experienced Bible teacher to facilitate and lead the Winning God's Way Mentoring Series. If someone asks you a question that you don't feel you can answer, just be honest and say you will try to find the answer, but you do not know, and move on.

Finally, the Winning God's Way Mentoring Series is written in such a format that I would encourage you to share your own stories or experiences in regard to the topic of each lesson.

Not only will this make you more comfortable but it will facilitate thoughts in those around you and they will begin to share.

FINAL THOUGHTS:

As the weeks go by, I would encourage you each week to send notes to athletes on their birthdays and also invite them to family gatherings so that they may see how a Christian acts at home. Also, the Winning God's Way study is written so that if someone does wish to begin attending after the meetings have started they may do so. It is not optimal but you don't want to limit God from working!

You will be richly blessed as you cover your group in prayer and see God working...thank you for helping further the kingdom!

WINNING Gods WAY

B R I E F   N O T E S   F O R   L E A D E R S
O N   W E E K L Y   L E S S O N S

Week 1 - GET WIRED

"Are you a Christian-athlete or an athlete that is a Christian?"
The purpose of this lesson is to assess where you are as a student-athlete both in and out of the athletic arena.

START: Have someone read John 15:5

Tips:
- *Dwell on the question:* Are you a Christian-athlete or an athlete that is a Christian? The difference being that an athlete that is a Christian thinks that when he/she steps on the court or field they can do and act however they want. This same person may not intentionally sin, but the heat of the battle causes them to do things they wish they hadn't and they apologize to God and everyone later. Conversely, a Christian-athlete sees things through Christ's eyes and is thinking like Christ and thinks before he or she acts. They see everything with an eternal significance.
- Talk about the fact that sometimes our body language, like turning our back on a teammate or rolling our eyes at a coach, speaks volumes.
- *Highlight Extra Point:* "You may be the only Bible your players ever read!"

How to Take Action:
➤ Romans 8:28 is a mechanism to get the athlete to stop, slow down and think before he or she acts. The scripture allows the Holy Spirit to speak to you and see things through Christ's eyes first as a Christian-athlete. Read Memory Verse.

WEEK 2 — THE TRAITS OF A WINNING GOD'S WAY

"What it takes to be the real deal"
This lesson will focus on being a servant leader, messenger and sent one. We will embrace the fact that in order to be the greatest, you must become the least.

START: Have someone read Titus 3:1-2

Tips:
➤ *Dwell on the question:* How do you model servant leadership to other players/family?
➤ Next move into what are the repercussions of them replicating your model. Can it help you win? Absolutely...we are only as strong as our weakest link right?
➤ You are also teaching the fact that no one is more important than anyone else. Humbleness—
➤ What about their families...are they being servants or being served? Help your parents!!
➤ Move down to The Challenge segment. The hardest thing for athletes to do is not have control. Competing is all about control. Control our opponent, the officials, and the game outcome.

God doesn't want us to just sit around and do nothing, but He does want us to trust Him and let Him work.

How to Take Action:
➤ Ask the athlete if they were the coach of their team how would they like their program to look ten years from now...now twenty. What impact can players have on leaving a legacy?
➤ Ask the athlete what type of program they want when they return ten years from now, because the young players of today are the starters of tomorrow! Read Memory Verse.

WEEK 3 — COMMITMENT TO EXCELLENCE

"What are my goals and how do I reach them?"
The purpose of this lesson is to discern Godly goals from worldly goals for a Christian athlete, and to help the athlete understand how to reach and measure those goals.

Start: Have someone read Matthew 6: 19-25

Tips:
➤ If you can, find some magazines or sports articles that glorify athletes and winning as the only thing that determines success in life. Show them to the group after you read the first paragraph of the lesson.
➤ Focus on the fact that it okay to have personal goals and to want to win, but God wants us to strive for goals that assure us eternal life and that further the kingdom.
➤ The 4 goals God wants for us in order are:
  1) An intimate Love relationship with Him
  2) Minister to your family
  3) Minister to your teammates
  4) Glorify God through your education and athletics
➤ You may want to ask the group why are the above Godly goals?
➤ When discussing their Training Regimen emphasize the importance of blocking out time with God and how important it is to be fresh. Morning time is the best, turn off the phone, and shut the door.
➤ Have people share different styles of quiet times and what works for others, but emphasize that all quiet time must involve the Word, prayer and watching and listening to God.

How to Take Action:
➤ Discuss the importance of spending time with God alone and how this will draw you closer to Him and you will then have the fuel you need to do His work. Read Memory Verse.

WEEK 4 - FEEDING THE MONSTER

"Is the schedule/sport eating you up...reset your priorities"
This lesson will focus on time management. We will discuss what a Christian-athlete's priorities look like and how a student-athlete can maintain balance within a hectic schedule.

Start: Have someone read Matthew 25:14-30, The parable of the talents was chosen because we want athletes to remember that God has given you many talents and gifts...the question: are you making the most of the gifts He has given you for the kingdom?

Tips:
➤ Have athletes share why they got into sports. When discussing if reasons have changed, bring up the fact that many athletes now play for a scholarship or for social status.
➤ Focus on the element of time and that all of us (especially athletes wish a day was 36 hours not 24.
➤ Discuss what unturned stones they have and are there any stones that could be left unturned or have God turn over for them.
➤ State that all of us shift around priorities based upon the importance of them at the time, but God wants us to keep things in perspective.
➤ Focus on the statement "How are you utilizing the time God has given you?"
➤ Emphasize that God can do more in 6 minutes that we can do in 6 months.
➤ *For added discussion:* What about the things athletes can't control...do they leave it up to God or do they worry and worry and waste time on them? Why?

How to Take Action: Have the athletes share their findings of listings their hours next to their priorities and discuss praying for God to help you utilize the time He has given us wisely. Read Memory Verse.

WEEK 5 — TAMING THE TONGUE

"Living a 'Playah's' lifestyle...the way God wants"
The purpose of this lesson is to help the athlete 'talk the talk and walk the walk' of a Christian-athlete on a daily basis.

Start: Have someone read James 3: 1-12, This is a long passage but is filled with great nuggets of information for the coach, beginning with the fact that teachers are judged more strictly and that praising and cursing come out of the same mouth. We can tame wild animals, control a huge ship with a small rudder but we cannot control our tongues. You are going to teach them today a way to compete and talk that will change them and their teammates forever. Instead of always criticizing and telling people what they are doing wrong, you are going to tell them what they are doing right and because they are so good at what they are doing they will do other great things in the future!

Tips:

➤ Focus on building your teammates up not tearing them down. The marine mentality works for a while but soon your teammates will not enjoy playing with you and or quit.

➤ Want to know the secret of getting your teammates to play at a high level... Remember, people don't care what you know until they know you care!

➤ When you speak greatness into someone, you speak a vision of greatness into his or her mind, i.e., "You are really improving, you are going to be the best shortstop to have ever played here."

➤ *The Put-up game:* During practice tell your yourself you have 10 minutes to give 3 other players on the team a sincere specific compliment, i.e., "Great hit Billy, you really drove that ball to right field well" or "Rick, I really appreciate how hard you work everyday even though you have not got to play much, thank you." It may sound hokey, but when people build each other up all the time it creates a climate of belief and positive attitudes that helps your team play better. Remember, happy players play better! You can also do the put ups following a practice or game with parents around to hear it. This has a huge impact on parents that don't see their children complaining, but instead lifting others up even after a loss!

➤ *Additional comment to share:* God is easy to please but hard to satisfy, we don't want blind obedience we want changed hearts in ourselves and teammates.

How to Take Action: Ask the athletes to THINK (acronym) before they speak but to also implement the "put up game" into their practices and games. Remember, don't compromise perfection but encourage your players! Read Memory Verse.

WEEK 6 — SEED PLANTERS

"Kids may not listen to their parents or teachers but they will listen to their friends!" This lesson will focus on the calling that we have as athletes for the kingdom of God to reach the generations of tomorrow.

Start: Have someone read Proverbs 22:6

Tips:

➤ Focus on the fact that we as athletes are called to glorify God through our play/actions.

➤ Lastly focus on the fact that some people in God's kingdom are planters, waterers, harvesters. Some people are only one, some two, and others all three or two of three. Ask the athletes to think where they fit in that model. Also remind them God can move them from category to category.

➤ Share what your harvest field looks like and ask other coaches to share what their fields look like.

➤ Share the importance and power of prayer and how God does the work if we pray.

➤ Have prayer be the primary supplement in the equation. Don't give up on friends or coaches.

How to Take Action: Emphasize the fact that it may take some seeds longer to sprout than others. State how friends sometimes come back years later thanking you for something you don't even remember saying or doing. Read Memory Verse.

WEEK 7 — CHECK YOUR OIL

"Character and Motives...making wise choices in difficult situations"
This lesson we will discuss the type of character and motivation God would like Christian-athletes to possess. We will also discuss the implications of character and motivation on an athlete's ability to make Godly choices and decisions.

Start: Have someone read John 8:1-11

Tips:
➤ Focus on question regarding the perception people have of you and how you can change that if you don't like it.

➤ Discuss the motivating factors that lead to decisions in the teen/athletic world, i.e., win at all costs, keep you starting position, please parents, please friends, don't like a teammate etc.

➤ Ask athletes if they go to the Father in Heaven for advice...First? If so, why do they or why should they?

➤ Spend the majority of the time talking about blind spots that we have and where we are vulnerable. We are all taught when driving to compensate for the blind spots in our mirrors by doing additional things like looking over our shoulder and checking other mirrors to insure safety. As Christian-athletes we have blind spots and we need to know what they are and how we can protect ourselves. Ask the athletes to make a list of their blind spots and how they can pray and take steps to protect themselves from harm.

How to Take Action: Read Memory Verse. Finish by talking about temptation and how our God is sovereign and if we allow Him to help us through prayer He will show us a way out. Trust the Word!

Reemphasize the importance of their quiet time each day.

WEEK 8 — THE DATING GAME

"Sex and Sports"
This purpose of this lesson is to help the athlete learn what God has to say about dating and sex in today's world and also to give the athlete Biblical principles and practice ways to handle the pressures of dating and sex.

Start: Have someone read 1 Thessalonians 4:3-5

Tips:
➤ Read first paragraph and then read 2 Corinthians 6:14-18.
➤ Focus on motivations for dating. Are your motivations Pure?
➤ What type of person does God want you to date and how?
➤ Ask and discuss how far is too far after reading the segment and Matthew 5:28, focus on the importance of communication prior to any intimacy in a relationship.
➤ If a person is not willing to respect your boundaries, you don't need that person in your life.

How to Take Action: Read Memory Verse. Finish by reviewing temptation and how our God is sovereign and if we allow Him to help us through prayer He will show us a way out. Then focus on describing what a relationship coach or coaches can do for you. Focus on the positives and that God wants us to have God honoring relationships. Remind them to set Godly boundaries.

WEEK 9 — BREAKFAST OF CHAMPIONS

"To supplement or not to supplement...that is the question!"
This purpose of this lesson is to discuss the use of supplements as a Christian-athlete and to also help the athlete develop a Biblically based process for determining whether or not they should use legal supplements.

Start: Have someone read 1 Corinthians 6:19-20

Tips:
➤ Read Jeremiah 29:11-13
➤ Focus on question regarding God's perception of taking supplements.
➤ Discuss the motivating factors that lead to the decision to consider taking supplements Are they from God?.
➤ Focus again on the body being a temple. You only get one Body!!!
➤ Talk about the fact that 30 years ago everyone thought steroids were harmless, but now we know the side affects. What about today's supplements... ephedrine used to be thought harmless and was legal now it is known to cause heart problems even death and is being taken off the shelves (discuss).

How to Take Action: Read Memory Verse. Go through the steps and go into more detail in how to hear God, you must be very close and have your antenna up. This comes from your quiet time and prayer with God. Remember, if it is not of God it is not from God!

WEEK 10 — MISSION POSSIBLE

"God's Purposes vs. Our Plans"
During this lesson we will discuss what God's purpose was in creating athletes and coaches. We will also learn how to align our plans with God's by utilizing the "Double Win" philosophy.

Start: Have someone read Proverbs 19:21

Tips:
➤ Focus on the question regarding what they think God's purpose is in having you as an athlete on His team.
➤ Ask why God created athletes and coaches and read aloud 1 Corinthians 9:22-23.
➤ Discuss the Double Win philosophy and ask them if they ever thought about what their overall philosophy is when competing. Lead them into the extra point note and writing a personal mission statement as an athlete, student and or friend.

How to Take Action: Go through the steps for making sure your plans align with God's purpose for you. If you have knowledge of Fasting principles it may be a good time to give a hand out or share verbally. Read Memory Verse.

WEEK 11 — HE'S CALLING YOU OUT

"Will you be a athlete God can use any way He wants?"
The purpose of this lesson is to show the importance of being obedient to God, in regard to the calling we have as both a Christian and an athlete. We will also discuss how one athlete can impact the world!

Start: Have someone read Philippians 2: 12-18 and tell the athletes that this morning they are going to be pushed to the edge of the cliff or to the edge of the nest. By the end of the lesson they will have decided in their heart if they are going to utilize and pass on the knowledge they now possess (competing and living with Biblical principles) and let God use them or not.

Tips:
➤ Focus on the question regarding what they think God's purpose is in having you as an athlete on His team. Lead them into the fact that a coach's favorite player is the most unselfish person on the team, that will do whatever is asked of them, without question. Immediate obedience.
➤ Discuss some ways athletes can be useful to God i.e., language, speaking opportunities, when people ask you why you do things the way you do, the media, etc.
➤ In discussing what it means to impact the infrastructure, reinforce that the purpose of the Winning God's Way series is to get them closer to God and to have them pass on what they now know and leave a legacy for the kingdom of God.

How to Take Action: Reinforce the fact that God has raised them up as athletes for such a time as this! Emphasize the fact that God uses ordinary people to do ordinary things! Read Memory Verse.

WEEK 12 - GET IN THE GAME

"More is caught than is Taught!"
The purpose of this lesson is to give the Christian-athlete practical and useful ways to leave a legacy for the kingdom of God in regard to style of play,

improving team chemistry, leading bible studies among your team, and servant leadership activities you can do on your campus and in your community.

Start: Have someone read Isaiah 49:6 and talk about the question; is it too much for God to ask us to do something for Him? Quick answer...No.

Tips:
➤ Simply follow what is written and for each heading share your own things you have done and have others share. The thrust of the lesson is to give them ideas and things they can do immediately to further God's kingdom and leave a legacy!

Finishing the Meeting:
➤ Finish by sending a sign up list around that includes the following:
➤ Who would like to do another Winning God's Way study next semester
➤ Who is going to start and lead a Winning God's Way study group in their school or community
➤ Who would like to purchase booklets for mentoring your athletes
➤ Who would like to become involved in a one on one mentoring program to go deeper

You will also have evaluations for them to fill out so you can better minister to their needs. Lastly, finish with a group prayer!

DESCRIPTION OF ACTIVITIES LISTED IN LESSON 12

"Create Memorable Experiences"
➤ Waiter/Waitress Day in Cafeteria (Have your players be greeters, waiters, busboys and servers in the school cafeteria. Brief them before hand that they are servant leaders and some people may not appreciate them, but don't worry about it and have fun with it. Then debrief them later as to how the experience as a servant felt and how people responded to their kindness and unselfishness. Also, discuss how the world does not understand why someone would help someone else for no apparent reason other than love.)
➤ Drink Servers at fast food restaurants (Call the restaurants ahead of time and tell what you are doing and make sure they understand that the athletes are not there to do work for the employees. Have your players stand by the drink machines and ask people if they can fill up their beverage for them. Again, brief your players before hand and tell them to accept no tips. When people are finished with their meal, have your players ask if they can take their trays to the garbage for them and

etc...Again, debrief and tie in the discussion to how unselfishness and servant leadership can make the world and your team a better place.)

➤ Operation Blessings (This is an activity that is broad in scope. This is where you as the coach decide how you can bless people in positions of servant hood, such as bus drivers, janitors, maintenance people, waiters, waitresses, cooks and also other teams on campus. Bus trips and team meals are great opportunities to bless people. At any time you the coach can present a t-shirt, hat, certificate or game ball to the bus driver, maintenance guys, or restaurant personnel. Follow each presentation with a team standing ovation or saying. Your team can do a watermelon feed for another team on campus. This really works great if a varsity team does it for a junior varsity or freshmen team. Again, emphasize the Biblical principle that the greatest among you must be a servant!)

➤ A Quality use of a Waste of Time (As coaches we developed these nights to promote a fun, competitive atmosphere and to keep our players close and out of trouble in the off-season. The only rule is that it must be fun, competitive and not related to the sport they play. We created old school gym nights where we played floor hockey on one side of the gym and kick ball on the other. Elementary school gym team games were always a big hit. We also played no dribble basketball and ultimate Frisbee along with a game of capture the flag. We had video scavenger hunts and some games from "Whose line is it anyway". We found that the kids loved being together and looked forward to the nights. It also allowed us to foster an atmosphere where competition is going on and teachable moments are plentiful. Your brainstorming will create memories your players will never forget. By the way we didn't debrief the kids after the activities, we would pray or do the put up game.

"More is Caught than is Taught"

➤ Start another Winning God's Way Mentoring program with your players

➤ Mentor a younger athlete (Encourage your athletes to consider spending time with a younger player one time per week and they can use the study they just went through with you.)

➤ Finish by sending a list around that includes:

➤ Who would like to do another Winning God's Way study next semester

➤ Who would like to start and lead a Winning God's Way study group on their team or among friends.

➤ Who would like to mentor a younger player in the future.

➤ Who would like to start, lead or join an FCA huddle on campus.

You will also have evaluations for them to fill out so you can better minister to their needs. Lastly, finish with a group prayer!